These are Frank Hildebrandt's words written over many years starting around the early '70's. Words and thoughts about the passing days of what came to his mind. They aren't in any special order, just inside for seeing the many years he felt at any given moment of time. Words sometimes on scraps of paper or a cocktail napkin. Saved for sharing to anyone's reading.

Some are written from his yearly Christmas cards sent to people that he has known over the years.

These may be his last writings!

Thoughts Along The Way

Frank Hildebrandt

Thoughts Along The Way

Copyright © 2025

All Rights Reserved

ISBN:

About the Author

For 46+ years, I've had a career in Law Enforcement. A dream I had since I was a little kid. Dreams sometimes do come true. Now that I am retired, I thought perhaps it was time to share these writings. So much time has passed. Most were written for someone special; shared, but most times not. Private thoughts that touched or were felt by me. Some did get shared, most not. Words were written down, hidden with some still sad. Most times, forgotten and filed away.

Never really forgotten.

Thoughts Along The Way

UNTITLED

May every door ahead,

open as you go.

And the ones you've

passed - stay ajar.

If for no other reason,

then to look back –

While always going on.

UNTITLED

Words that never

      will be spoken.

Are sounds that

      never will be heard.

Letters that never

      will be written.

Are thoughts that

      never will be read.

UNTITLED

There is a time for laughter,

    and there is a time for tears,

for each of us has happy days,

    and days when grief appears.

But we have our troubles,

    just as when we're glad and gay,

we should always remember,

    that this, too, will pass away.

Thoughts Along The Way

THE "GG" TRAIN (QUEENS OF BROOKLYN)

The ride
was longer than usual.
I felt it would last,
beyond the time
I had remaining.
To be late,
the excuse
couldn't be told.

Lights flash by.
It's late. No,
the sun hasn't risen.

I'm alone
this morning.
I felt it when I left.
My head still filled

there's nothing inside.

LOOK BACK

Sometimes,
    as we pass
        through this life
    a person catches
        a passing smile
            as we move by.

Thoughts are exchanged,
    then passed back.
As they entangle
    the closeness becomes
        apparent

    But, life
        with a pace that
cannot stand still
    allows each person

       many paths.

Roads to nowhere, yet
  ever moving to somewhere.
And yes,
  sometimes back to
    the beginning...

the smile.

August 1985

HER EYES

When I look
    and see you
        looking,
your eyes show me
    something unique
        for the first time.

Perhaps, it's the
    way you're able
  to let me know
the feelings enclosed.
Maybe it's not intended
    to show feeling
        to me,
  but

        I hope to

  grasp the glance,

even for that
           brief second.

Please look back.

I never looked
    away.

Thoughts Along The Way

August 1985

THE ESCAPE

An affair

    is something

        I use

for the journey.

The journey

    which I have

taken before,

        and

    returned alone.

Unsure,

    I need the thought

        you're coming.

Don't ask,

    I don't know the course.

What I purpose

Thoughts Along The Way

        is uncertainty

            that

I'll ever escape.

Let's draw a map.

February 1987

THE WEEKEND

Did I say
    thank you?
It seems
    we steal,
for the weekends
    from a week
        of lost treasures.
We take each
    others dreams
        into a single
            move.

Moving forward
    in the discovery
of the end — and

Thoughts Along The Way

beginning of the
    search
        through
another week,
        for a glimpse
of the thought
        a weekend,
    will come
        again....
And again.

UNTITLED

I'm in love
       with a dream.
Not so much
          with you,
     as the thought
        of you.
I know it's not love
but, I grasp for
        the dreams
    of a man in love.
Not with love.
I'll always dream,
     of you.

UNTITLED

A year passes
> with a bunk
>> of an eye.

Only by
> keeping them
>> open,
can I slow time.

I just haven't learned,
> to dream with
>> open eyes.

UNTITLED

As I pass AMCH
>her memory is
>>felt.

I know she
>wasn't always mine
>but, there was
>>a time I thought
>>>she was.

Deep inside me her
>love is there.

Now as I walk
>>>>by,
>thinking only of
>>the many times

I was here.

In my memories,
   she will
      always be mine.

I now share her,
      with no one.

UNTITLED

When,

   I try to talk

       with my feelings,

you never understand.

Do I expect

       too much

   from a relationship

          with you?

I'm trying

       to be more open,

  than you're

          able to accept.

Maybe,

  maybe not.

I took you

       as a precious stone.

MY BIRTHDAY

Next year

      I'll spend it different.

Only each year

has become

      a repeat,

           of the ones past.

Next year,

I'll spend it different.

March 1989

YOU MY FRIEND

S̲ome people
> come into
>> our lives

and leave,
> leaving us with
>> many memories.

You my friend,
> have

left me
> much to remember.

Memories,
> which tomorrow
>> we can

remember…..
> You and I.

YESTERDAY GONE BY

Yesterday's belong
      to one's past.
You can go back,
      but you cannot
     live ---
          time gone by.
Use your dreams
      to relive your memories
  of the days
      that have gone
          by.
Life is meant
      to be lived for today
  which is to become,
         tomorrow.

GIRAFFES

Giraffes are able

    to reach much

higher than I.

  Unlike the

giraffes, I didn't understand

the extent of my reach.

I respect that, but

  don't understand

      why …..

Thoughts Along The Way

THE AIRPORT

Moving through

    the airport

I feel alone.

People rush to

    lines, few smile

only to wait.

Planes come

    and go.

New people rush

    by. All

going somewhere. Some

    going nowhere.

What seems

    to be the same?

As we fly

Thoughts Along The Way

    from this place

        to that.

I had a plan

        or thought.

We expect and

    surely know

        no such plan

will always follow through.

I had a plan,

    what happened?

THE PASSING OF A DAISY

Now it's winter.

Cold, silent, lonely -----
    as I look out
        into the fields,
  snow covers the ground.

As sure as spring rains
        she will be back.
Reaching higher,
    greener than blades
           of grass.
Grasping the yellow
        in the golden sun ----
  she will still retain,
        the white of
    winter's edge.

Thoughts Along The Way

Calling to her
        now,
                through
the howling winter
        winds.
She will not respond
      to my voice.

She follows
      not me,
    she is too gentle
to fight the wind.
        But,
Spring is near.

The rain will replace
      the snow,
   the wind will pass.

    Passing on winter

to spring,

    she will come.

The sun will lift

    her into the air.

Drops of rain warmed

  by the sun, moves

  her into life.

Each day a little closer

  yet, nearer to

    when she will go.

The rains have stopped

  and the suns light,

  lets me see her.

Summer is the time

    she enjoys most.
      Watching her beauty now
          is hard to hold.

If I grasp her gentle
    frame, she will die.
But, leaving her there
      winter will again take
        her away.

Summer must give way
    to Fall.
Should I let her fade
   into the winter wind,
     or
       take hold
now, and hope?

Maybe

    if I gave her love

        she would not die.

The winter will take

    her back.

I'll reach out

  again

    for her.

If the winter takes her

  before I reach the fields,

    she will be gone.

Maybe she will come again

        and again

But, somehow I think -----

    this **Daisy**, may not.

The fields are

  within sight.

Feeling chilled,
   my heart now subtle
  by the coming wind
     that winter always
          brings.

Just this once,
    couldn't winter
 be late….

UNTITLED

Now,

for the second time

I find myself alone.

Alone in a time

when a man needs

a warm hand, a

tender touch, understanding,

but most of all

love.

Man can not

exist without it,

nor should he try.

I look within every woman,

but never find the

complete person I want.

Could it be I ----- who
must change.
Some have said yes,
many have said no.
I think not.

I want what is felt.
It's the feeling that
is not right..

I could give, if----
only you were right.

I will keep looking,
but how long will it take?
Maybe that question is
 incorrect or words wrong.

Thoughts Along The Way

I know time as a measurement
does not apply----I have
to put it another
way.

Which way?

UNTITLED

For each day we live

there will have been

    a yesterday.

Remember each day vividly

    forgetting

        not the smallest detail.

Don't allow the

    tomorrow's ahead----

To be empty of dreams

        of the days gone by.

Thoughts Along The Way

THE LETTER THAT NEVER CAME

I waited for your letter.

No, it hasn't come

yet ---- maybe tomorrow.

She will surely send

a Christmas card ---- she's

good that way you know.

DISCARDED TREASURES

W alking along the beach

    I see how life

        moves along

the water's edge.

Washing in upon

    the shore

  then out ---- leaving

        treasures to be found,

discarded by the sea.

Some are again reclaimed

        and lost,

  most again

    discarded by the sea.

Thoughts Along The Way

Treasures for those of us
        who seek them
to be saved in another
        corner of our world.

Only later
        to be discarded
    and just maybe .....
                again reclaimed.

UNTITLED

Sadness never seems
> to totally end
> these last few years.

I must put together
> my life
> to reach a
> point of living.

The thought of
> giving up, is
> considered more often.

What sanity I still possess
> keeps me moving.

If that little bit

was to be drained

now ----

The struggle would

be over.

UNTITLED

As I am
- greeted by the
  - sun

the desire for
- living becomes

more evident.

If only the
- sun could shine,

everyday.

WINDY NIGHT

As I sit,

    passing time

        with the wind,

the night brings

        moments of loneliness.

The feeling felt,

    when you move from

        my eyes.

I look for you

  and know you're safe,

    but not within my

        reach.

You're like the wind.

Thoughts Along The Way

Moving away, then back.

When you're near

   the warmth holds

         me within your arms.

 As you let go

   the wind returns --

let go as you must

   but, come back to me

         before the night

   gives way.

UNTITLED

I have chosen

        my profession….

You have trained

        me well….

We have given

        our best….

Now dear lord

        give me rest.

UNTILTED

Moments are

no longer moments.

They've come

together and

now---years

have passed.

Time builds

more distance,

then miles could

ever hope to do.

We can not move

back in time,

but miles can

be overcome.

Run this way----

and hope.

UNTITLED

M_y life

    seems to reach

        for more

            then I can find.

Why ----

    after all these

        years,

    haven't I been

    able to settle?

It's as if

    I am lost,

somewhere between

    yesterday and today.

Tomorrow will have

to bring the answer,

or the end.

UNTITLED

How do you say

to someone,

"I am losing you"?

Or perhaps

that's wrong, because

I have lost you.

Maybe not to him

or even the one

before that.

It's

more likely to be,

the one tomorrow.

And that,

not even I can stop

nor you.

But that lost,

if even recovered,

would never belong----

To me.

LAST NIGHT

Last night
    wasn't easy,
and this morning
    was even worse.

Tomorrow morning
    hasn't come,
maybe it will stay away
    just this once.

UNTITLED

You remember the dreams

        I had that first

    day we met?

They say

    it's good to dream you know.

I'm not so sure,

    sometimes they're just

        Dreams.

UNTITLED

Loneliness

    of unbearable magnitude

        has entered my life.

Far greater then

    even I

        had anticipated,

  or

knew possible.

Now,

    unable to deal

        with it,

    I must act.

I find myself lost.

Never have I

seen life,

so empty.

January 1978

THE SUN .... IS SHE

The sun
   seems to give way
to allow me
     another day.

I think back
   wondering why,
the last moments
     moved by so rapidly?

Then it's over.

It's recaptured,
        loved
again

lost to the night.

Now,

    with a mere blink

  of my eyes

    my memories

        hold

           the sun.

If only

  for that once,

  why couldn't….

        No.

Like the sun

    she

  will always come

    and will always go.

Tomorrow

   I know the sun

      will come again.

THE TORTOISE AND THE LADY

Life, comes and goes.

Each day passes

with time moving,

unable to slow

to my pace.

I have not known

the speed of others.

My motion slow,

as I wander with

the journey of time.

Somehow in the journey

the nearness of others,

a stranger to me.

Upon my shoulders

I struggle, with the

burden of my life.

Thoughts Along The Way

It's not easy

traveling slowly and alone.

She must have needed

a place to rest,

and I, her touch.

Now she, no added

burden to my life.

Rides with me,

through the journey

 of time.

UNTITLED

Listen,

    I'm here.

    Don't leave me yet.

        Where do I go?

        How do I pay?

1977

SHE DOESN'T KNOW

Who is he?

I can't make him go,
nor let him stay.

I can't put him down,
nor pick him up.

Yet,
why is he here?

I should know.
He knows.

Why not me?
Frank why?

UNTITLED

I plea for life

for death is close.

I can see it

yet, I can't look.

It's felt by me.

But, yet untouched.

It's here ---- next to me.

My breath short.

Darkness fills my eyes,

I no longer see.

My hand motionless

it's ended.

I'm dead.

UNTITLED

If man -----

Was to stop,

life is said to end.

UNTITLED

Listen to the sounds.

It's like you can feel

the chill, and

not merely the wind.

UNTITLED

I look back

at life

one could say,

to remember.

Life is made

of memories.

What was past

and what will pass.

Today somehow

leaves me to believe,

that my memories

lie within that past.

THE APARTMENT

Days have passed

since I was there.

I drove by today

only to remember yesterday,

or was it

the day before?

Time passes and we forget

somehow I remember.

Everyone sees the sign

"Apartment for Rent."

I was there, but

then so was she

at **255**.

Thoughts Along The Way

UNTITLED

As sure as the sun
    comes up each
  morning,
another day will
  get a new
    beginning.

YOU AND I ARE DIFFERENT.

It's hard to believe..

I'm not sure why

I guess,   no.

Maybe I'm different.

I would think

if only people would look.

You must be different.

To be the same

you see nothing,

outside your vision.

I want to see

beyond the farthest mountain.

To use only one's eyes

you lack the difference,

between you and I.

UNTITLED

As I find myself
    sad and lonely,
I just think
    about the days
        gone by.

I possess
    the power
  to recall all
    my yesterdays.
Reliving them
    one by one
  in my mind.

The reason is
    we are alive.
  And there will always

be a tomorrow.

So today,
   will become a yesterday
      that can be remembered,
         or
just forgotten.

But never forget -----

There will always
     be memories,
   of the tomorrow's ahead.

UNTITLED

Today, as yesterday

will never be reclaimed.

For once something

is gone

this perhaps, is

when we must find

something in its place.

Love too becomes

lost, but we somehow

someway replace that.

But, in the replacement

what was passed

is still there.

For-----

Love that is received

is never truly forgotten!

UNTITLED

If,

I was to touch

you again.

I'm sure it would

be the same.

Remembering --- the parts

that were made

to be touched.

And the parts,

made only to be

held---

The handle bars ---------

UNTITLED

Sometimes,

there comes a time

when people need.

And, with each need

want someone. And

with this want,

which may come

at any time.

Seems to come

at the end,

Christmas is said

to come at the

end,

of December.

So this Christmas,

I need and want

you.

Thoughts Along The Way

I'm people----

UNTITLED

A birthday---

Which comes once

in any given year.

Is never remembered

by many, other

than the person

forgotten.

More than not,

it is remembered.

But,

not at the right time.

So I send this card today

for the many

Happy Birthday's of

Thoughts Along The Way

yesterday----

SEEDS

If we were

to collect -----

A few seeds everyday,

and save them

until it rains.

On that day,

we could start

from the beginning.

Each seed has

the power of life.

So life can start

when we begin.

UNTITLED

I find it hard

to remember.

Not of you,

which is something

that can't be

forgotten. But ------

Of the last time

we touched.

It seems to be

such a long time ago -----

THE LOSS OF A DAISY

I passed by the field
        and thought of you.
Never have I seen
            so many before.

Could I hold
        the beauty I could see?

As I made my way
        I wanted to grasp
each and every one.

I tried as you see,
            but
none are mine.

Take what I have
seen. They are yours.

I remember
    each time I pass,
but a single one.
    Or by just
        thinking of you.

UNTITLED

As I find myself

      sad and lonely,

I just think

  about the days

        gone by.

I possess

  the power

to recall all

      my yesterdays.

Reliving them

    one by one

  in my mind.

The reason is

    we are alive.

  And there will always

        be a tomorrow.

So today,
   will become a yesterday
      that can be remembered
         or
just forgotten.

But never forget---

There will always
     be memories,
of the tomorrows ahead.

January 31, 2006

WHERE HAVE THE FLOWÉRS GONE?

T he Flowérs
    have come
        and gone…

We had, but
    a short time
        to watch them grow.

I got to know,
    her smile
    for too short
        of time.

No one knows
    just how long

Thoughts Along The Way

       Flowérs will

            grow.

Perhaps if we

      let them go

          wild

              on their own,

they could survive.

No one knows

      just how long

           Flowérs will

                grow.

I had thought

      that,

   that this Flowér

             won't die.

She gave me

so much joy,

   in the colors

      of her

         smile.

"… do you know

     how much I love

        you?..." seemed

   to be

what echoed from

       her smile.

How did the

   sunshine

leave us so soon?

No one knows

   just how long

      Flowérs will

        grow.

Thoughts Along The Way

For my wife,

Marléne Michael who

was always my Flowérs

CONTENTS:

1985: It's cold, and Christmas

1985: Glimpse of Christmas past

1986: The night before

1986: Christmas revealed

1988: Christmas magic

1990: For yet another year

1991: Searching at Christmas

1994: A gift for Christmas

1994: Christmas back then

1995: Christmas lights

1998: Toys **R** us

1998: Changing colors

1999: Ice crystals

2002: The wreath on the door

2003: The Christmas card

2004: The creek

1985

IT'S COLD, AND CHRISTMAS

The snow has
    started
  and the night has come,
lying across the sky
      as a cold blanket.

I feel chilled,
    seeing the wind
  blow the snow against
      my window.
Looking out into the
    winter's night
  I think of so many
      moments…
    yet past,

   and some that
 I hope to come.

It's Christmas,
  and the snow
    is most welcome tonight.

People are locked inside
   with friends,
  loves and loves that might
     have been,
  but never will.

I dream upon
    each snowflake
  and watch them disappear
     within the night sky,
 only to be rebuilt
    upon the ground.

Thoughts Along The Way

I now drift,
    as with the snow.
  Drift as we may tonight
      upon the snow
in front of our eyes
      memories fade,
blending amidst the snow
      then only to be set
        adrift,
    by the wind.

Behind my window
    the wind reminds me
      it's cold, and Christmas.

People are locked inside
      with friends,
loves and loves that might
      have been,

but never will.

1985

GLIMPSE OF CHRISTMAS PAST

T he ground is
> covered with
>> snow.
> As I walk and
>> remember
> years back,

Christmas was so
> much different
>> back then.

Windows are dressed
> with lights blinking
>> a warm welcome
> as I pass by.

Inside one catches

  a glimpse of faces,

    smiles and friends.

As I stand

  staring,

 I feel warm

  as the wind blows

   against my face.

It's cold,

 and as the snow

  falls,

 I'm reminded I must

   move on.

Down the road

  home waits,

   and it's Christmas.

Thoughts Along The Way

1986

THE NIGHT BEFORE

The sun
   moves down
making way for the
   evening stars.

The night is chilled,
     with
   the light snow
that falls upon my
      face.

The rush of people
    leaving the
       stores,
  pushing past

with the last

minute treasures.

As I walk,

    the familiar bell

        is ringing.

The little woman dressed

    in red

requesting a bit of

        sharing,

that comes with Christmas.

The snow is a little

    heavier now,

as it builds under

        each step.

A little closer to

    home,

where one will find

    the outstretched arms

of friends and loves

    we will share,

this Christmas

    season with.

1986

CHRISTMAS REVEALED

As I sit,

    my eyes

        once again

    gaze into the

        fireplace.

I ponder,

        as I watch

    the fire flicker.

The familiar smells

        of Christmas

    fill the air.

Slowly drifting,

I imagine
>the thoughts
of Christmas morning.

Packages being opened,
>the anticipation of
>>discovering dreams,
>the disappointment of
>>forgotten hopes.

Thinking back,
>thoughts
>>of so many years
>>>drift past.

As the fire crackles,
>I'm brought
>>back.

Tomorrow is Christmas.
>And

so come the dreams

                and hopes

  we will discover,

this Christmas season.

1988

CHRISTMAS MAGIC

As I turned
　　another page,
　　　　drifting
　　the book
　　　　I held
　　　　　　felt heavy,
　　as I
　　　　was
　　　　　　made
　　　　warm by
　　　　　　the
　　　　　　　　fire.

My mind turned
　　from the printed pages,

Thoughts Along The Way

    to the thoughts

        of Christmas.

Christmas for most,

    had started.

Not much like

    years ago,

when we thought

    Santa Claus brought

        the MAGIC,

the boxes under

    the trees,

and the joy

    in people's hearts.

I guess I fell

    asleep

in this old soft chair.

    But,

I seem to remember

the lights on the

        tree were out.

And those gifts---

As I looked up

    rubbing my eyes,

        I saw her smiling.

"It's MAGIC," she said

        with a smile

                and a ho ho ho.

I knew then,

    as long as

        one believes,

    Christmas is the MAGIC

        within all of

            us.

Thoughts Along The Way

1990

FOR YET ANOTHER YEAR

The smell of

    pine has faded

    for yet another year.

The holidays have passed,

    and we remember

    the excitement which was

        built into a

    single morning.

Perhaps it's good Christmas

    comes but once a year.

        Leaving us with

    undisappointed dreams

    lasting throughout the year.

Oh yes, just as we
>> move through
> the months until the
>>> magic comes back,
> we shall not forget.

The reminders are found,
> rediscovered, lost
> within the many corners
of our lives.

The glimmer is unmistaken.

That piece of tinsel
> curled in that corner,
>> overlooked, forgotten.
Tucked away with those
> undisappointed dreams.

And,

    left in place

        for yet another year.

1991

SEARCHING AT CHRISTMAS

W here was it that

    we went

        in search of a tree?

I remember that walk

    so long ago.

The December air hinted

        that Christmas was near.

The cold wasn't felt then,

        only the thoughts

            of Christmas.

We made our way

    and somehow knew,

    which one to cut.

Does it always happen
    that way?

That tree was long ago
    discarded,
  that Christmas
    has passed years of others,
and now,
    to another…

We no longer walk
    through those woods
in search of a tree.

We found it that year.

I guess I did discover
    many things then.

Just what they were

    are now left to memories.

I wonder if people

    still do that,

    search for a tree?

Thoughts Along The Way

1994

A GIFT FOR CHRISTMAS

In and out
    of the stores,
we search
    to discover the joy,
that one special offering
    to share with another
        and another.

What is it,
    that makes us search endlessly
        until we find it?
    Do we ever find
        that special gift
            of sharing?

Thoughts Along The Way

Maybe it's really out
        in the open.
Perhaps inside our thoughts
           or
    wrapped within
        our hearts.

Gifts at Christmas
    are not always within paper.
        To be unwrapped with hands
           paper discarded.

    Most times,
they're stored within us.
    Shared,
  given away
      and maybe taken back.

The real gifts
    at Christmas

are always within us.

Passed with a mere glance,

   a spoken word,

      a smile.

It's not for sale,

   held or

      unwrapped.

It's felt between us.

1994

CHRISTMAS BACK THEN

It's not yet morning,

    it's dark,

the light hasn't crept in

    between the curtain

        openings.

The windows always seemed

    to have had frost on them.

        I remember our windows

        had shades.

    Did they have window blinds

        back then?

My brother slept

    below me

      on the lower bunk.

          My sister

        in the other room,

           no others.

They came later,

    my little brother

           and sister.

None of that mattered

        back then

    not even the cold

        linoleum floors.

           Did everyone

        have linoleum?

It was okay then

    to get up early

        or

    at least

we were not scolded for long.

Thoughts Along The Way

Christmas came

      and went back then

  as it does for most kids.

Searching through

    my mind,

I can't remember much more

      about those mornings---

  Rice Krispies and milk

and my feet

    on the cold linoleum floors.

1995

CHRISTMAS LIGHTS

The leaves
   aren't quite covered
      yet.

The colors still
   shine
      through
   the snow,
      almost
   melting the flakes
      as they fall.

The cold and wind
      have stayed away,
         the snow

Thoughts Along The Way

  tries to build

     a blanket

  to hide

what the trees gave away.

We always wish

     for the snow

  this day, but

I'm glad the leaves

     won.

The colors feel

  so much warmer

     now,

  more like lights

glimmering among the trees.

Thoughts Along The Way

1998

TOYS R US

D_o you really

    think

   Christmas is about

     toys?

I think I thought
  that. At least
at one time I did.

I learned
  the true meaning
    of Christmas,
  way back then.
I mean I know,
  but the toys

were Christmas.

I haven't received
   any toys in many years,
I don't even believe
     I still have any.

Does someone
   give them back
     or, do they just
        disappear?

I wouldn't want that---
     you know,
   the disappearing part.

I guess I should
     just believe that
   Christmas is magic.

The magic that comes

        and goes within us.

    It doesn't need

        to be real,

    imaginary

        or even seen.

Just as long as you—

    believe.

Never let it disappear

    no matter where

        the toys **R**.

1998

CHANGING COLORS

Walking,

    the leaves crunch

        under the weight

            of my feet.

    The sounds,

we've grown to know.

On this clear day,

    as the bright sun

        shines through

    the trees,

the reds, yellows, oranges, greens

    color my thoughts.

For sure,

winter
> lies ahead.

The leaves will
> give way
> and the snow
>> will fall.

The shy has changed
> and the blowing wind,
has moved the colors
>> behind doors.

Inside, the trees
> are green
covered by the color
>> of lights and dreams.
They replace the fallen
> leaves
>> reds, yellows, oranges…

Thoughts Along The Way

I'll miss the fall,

    as I always do.

        But,

            it gives us

    the winter.

Passing into spring,

    with a short

    stop at Christmas.

A brief moment in time,

    between the

        changing colors.

1999

ICE CRYSTALS

The rains have
        slowed,
      to that faint drizzle
         my face
can't escape.

The cold holds the drops
      that freeze, building
  as they land
         on the ground.

The snow becomes entombed
      with no escape. Covered,
        guarded, protected
by the frozen mist.

Ice Crystals crack

        under my very

                steps.

As the sun's

        light struggles,

    stealing the sky…

The ice won.

Covered,

    the glitter takes over

        once the rain

            passes.

For the moment,

    we succumb in awe,

        to the **"Ice Crystals."**

Thoughts Along The Way

2002

THE WREATH ON THE DOOR

The smell in

    the air,

  is just about gone.

Needles

    have already started

        falling.

Opening the door,

    the wind blowing

  dropping them to my feet.

Weeks ago,

    the smell came

        back

    I looked for that hook

    realizing,

there never was.

A way is found,

        captured

                but,

a promise never kept.

Each year,

     meaning to get something,

         planning

            and

    each year waiting

       for the next.

The smell again

        will return.

  Needles fall

      as the wind blows

         in the open door.

Each year,

    looking to the next…

As the door is closed,

        the smell is gone.

2003

THE CHRISTMAS CARD

Little snow

    is forecasted,

        as I walk

to the box.

Most days,

        this time

            of year,

it's easy to be

            reminded

        of friends,

           family

and so much more.

You sort through

the pile

    you hold

looking, reading

   and

      figuring out

those return addresses.

Who sent them,

    who remembered,

        who didn't,

and those that

   couldn't, but

     you remember.

The cards are

   the way we

      remember,

  and will remember

     and remember…

Thoughts Along The Way

2004

THE CREEK

Earlier today

    the sounds

        could be heard.

Water running

        as it flows

    over the rocks.

The snow from the trees

    dropping in clumps,

melting,

    adding to the sounds.

The creek is usually

    frozen by 'Christmas'

most years.

Sounds heard
   at winter's end.

A tree had fallen
   from winters back.
The weight
   of a storm,
      long past.

They say
   the cold weather
      isn't
         far away.

Perhaps!

Tomorrow
     the creek

will slow again,

      freeze…

and 'Christmas' comes,

      the day after that.

Thoughts Along The Way

Thoughts Along The Way

www.ingramcontent.com/pod-product-compliance
Lightning Source LLC
LaVergne TN
LVHW051038070526
838201LV00066B/4852